THE SCIENCE OF GYM CLASS

More Than Just Dodgeball and Sweatpants

By Darlene R. Stille

COMPASS POINT BOOKS
a capstone imprint

Compass Point Books
1710 Roe Crest Drive
North Mankato, MN 56003

Editors: Sarah Eason and Geoff Barker
Designers: Paul Myerscough and Geoff Ward
Media Researcher: Susannah Jayes
Content Consultant: Harold Pratt, President, Educational Consultants Inc.
and Science Curriculum Inc.
Production Specialist: Laura Manthe

Image Credits
Alamy: James Nesterwitz 45 t, PCN Photography 15, Jeff Rotman 28 b, Michael Ventura 34 r;
Capstone Studio: Karon Dubke 6–7, 12–13, 16–17, 25, 31, 42–43, 51, 54–55, 58–59; **Corbis:**
epa/Paul Miller 61 t, Reuters/Matt Sullivan 19 b; **Geoff Ward:** 9, 10 b, 29, 37; **Shutterstock:**
2265524729 44 b, Andresr 52 b, Apollofoto 3, 53, 56 b, 63, Noam Armonn 11, ayakovlev.com
48 b, 49 l, Galina Barskaya 14 b, Bedov 24 b, Olga Besnard 40 br, Blamb 32 r, Yanik Chauvin
56 tl, 60 tl, Andrea Danti 23, Zhu Difeng 27 b, Bojan Dzodan 26 b, Jose Gil cover bgd, 19 t,
28 m, 40 m, 61 b, Andreas Gradin 39 b, Alan C. Heison 30 b, Jiang Dao Hua 36 t, 38 tl, 40 tl,
44 tl, 46 tl, Ken Inness 50 b, Herbert Kratky 35, Dmytro Larin 46 r, Reistlin Magere 41, Monkey
Business Images 21, Andril Muzyka 20 b, Vitalii Nesterchuk 48 tl, 50 tl, 52 tl, Khoroshunova
Olga 22 r, Kruglov Orda back cover, 14 t, 18 tl, 20 tl, 22 tl, 24 tl, Edyta Pawlowska 4 br,
Poulsons Photography 39 t, Prodakszyn 47, Pavel Reband 5, Francesco Ridolfi 33 b, Pete
Saloutos 45 b, Howard Sandler 57, Sergielev 4 tl, 8 tl, 10 tl, Igor Stepovik 38 b, Jason Stitt 18
b, 26 t, 28 tl, 30 tl, 32 tl, 34 tl, 60 b, Supri Suharioto 27 t, Mike Tan C. T. 49 r, Tankist276 36
b, the24studio cover, URRRA 33 tc, Luna Vandoorne 1, 8.

This book was manufactured with paper containing
at least 10 percent post-consumer waste.

Library of Congress Cataloging-in-Publication Data
Stille, Darlene R.
  The science of gym class: more than just dodgeball and sweatpants /
by Darlene R Stille.
      p. cm.—(Everyday science)
  Includes index.
  ISBN 978-0-7565-4485-0 (library binding)
  ISBN 978-0-7565-4504-8 (paperback)
  1. Sports sciences—Juvenile literature. 2. Physical education and
training—Juvenile literature. 3. Performance—Juvenile literature. I. Title.
  GV558.S75 2012
  613.7'1—dc23   2011015249

Visit Compass Point Books on the Internet at *www.capstonepub.com*

Printed in the United States of America in North Mankato, Minnesota.
042012
006691R

table of
contents

more than just dodgeball

What's the point of trying to hit someone with a ball or dodging when a player throws the ball at you? Is this a silly game—a waste of school time? Not at all, says your gym teacher. Neuroscientists, who study the brain and nervous system, and kinesiologists, who study movement, all agree.

You require balance for every move you make—even carrying the groceries!

Steady!

Playing dodgeball helps to develop your sense of balance. You need a good sense of balance to do such fun things as riding a bike and rollerblading, as well as things that aren't so much fun, such as helping your mom carry the groceries from the store. Balance improves your eye-hand coordination—and your eyes and hands must work together to do more than play video games. Eye-hand coordination is needed for such skills as sewing a patch on your jeans or pounding a nail in the wall to hang a picture. Dodgeball and other games improve your reflexes by teaching your body to respond instantly, without even thinking, when an object comes speeding your way. Good reflexes are essential for responding to real-life emergencies, such as making a sudden stop or turning fast to avoid an accident when driving a car.

It might seem like play, but the skills you learn in gym class can help you lead a safer, healthier life.

Test Your Reflexes

You will need:

- 12-inch (30-cm) ruler
- A partner

1. Hold the ruler with your thumb and forefinger, at the end marked 12 inches (30 cm).

2. Let the ruler hang down. Ask your partner to hold his or her hand at the other end of the ruler, but without touching it.

3. Tell your partner that you are going to drop the ruler within the next 5 seconds. Your partner must catch the ruler with one hand as fast as he or she can.

4. Count down five, four, three . . . Let the ruler go at some point during the countdown.

5. Record the level in inches or centimeters at which your partner catches the ruler.

6. Repeat the experiment three times, varying the time when you let go of the ruler.

7. Switch places and repeat the experiment. Ask an adult to try the experiment too.

The person who catches the ruler farthest from the 12-inch (30-cm) mark has the fastest reflexes.

5

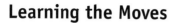

Learning the Moves

Gym class is more like math or science class than you may think. In math and science you read, memorize facts, and apply what you learn to solve problems. Learning mainly involves your brain. In gym class learning involves both your brain and your body. It teaches your body how to move.

Learning in all subjects involves your nervous system. Your nervous system is like a vast network of wires running all over your body. The brain is the control center of the nervous system. The wires are your nerves—thin cells that send signals to your brain. Your brain takes in all the information from your nerves and decides what to do with it. If your brain decides that you need to run away from danger, it sends signals through the nerves that tell the muscles in your legs to move.

A dance move feels instinctive, but your brain has sent many messages to your body to instruct muscles, bones, and joints to carry out the move.

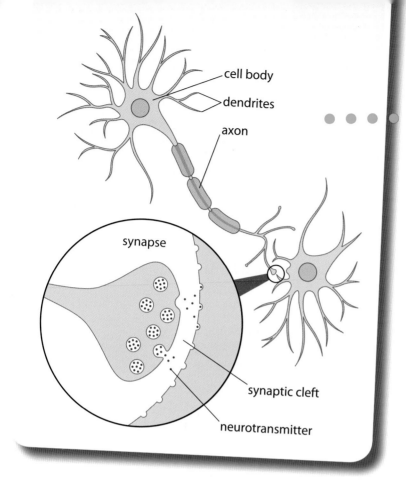

cell body

dendrites

axon

synapse

synaptic cleft

neurotransmitter

If you think your computer is powerful, think again! Your brain is a powerhouse of neurons, all busily sending messages to each other via neurotransmitters to tell your body what to do.

Command Center

The average adult human brain weighs about 3 pounds (1.4 kilograms). It looks like a wobbly mass of pinkish-gray jelly, covered with grooves and ridges. The brain is like a powerful computer, but it doesn't have a big screen, keyboard, joystick, and other fancy controls. Except it has much more computing power than the fastest microchips around today.

Computer chips process computer code, written in millions of zeros and ones. Your brain has about 100 billion nerve cells, called neurons. Fifty trillion connections, called synapses, link the neurons. The neurons send out signals. Electrical and chemical signals move along nerve fibers that link all the neurons in your body. Your brain can also form new connections between neurons. The connections form when you learn a new skill, such as remembering a fact or riding a bike.

9

Parts of the Brain

The cerebrum is the largest and most complex part of your brain. The neurons in the cerebrum help you to see, hear, feel, think, and learn. The smaller cerebellum looks after your sense of balance. It takes in information from your senses and coordinates this information with the movements of your muscles. Neuroscientists think that learning movements involved in gym class happens in your cerebellum. In learning how to swim, skate, or throw a ball, your brain remembers what the movement feels like.

Study of Movement

The science behind gym is called kinesiology, the study of movement. Kinesiologists study all kinds of movement involved in work, sports, dance, and play. Some kinesiologists teach physical fitness or coach sports. Others do scientific research in biochemistry, physiology, and sports medicine. Kinesiologists work in all kinds of places, including elementary and high schools, colleges and universities, hospitals and medical clinics, private companies, and the military.

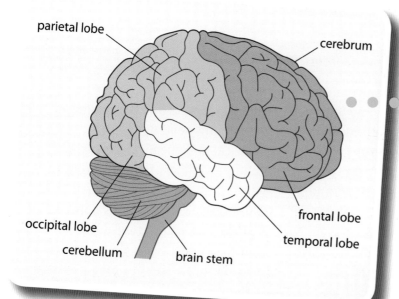

parietal lobe

cerebrum

occipital lobe

cerebellum

brain stem

frontal lobe

temporal lobe

The cerebellum is found at the back of your brain. It is from here that the messages that tell your body how to move are sent.

Your body and brain work together to help you learn how to swim.

It Takes Practice

Your brain and body work closely together to learn all kinds of movements, from riding a bike to throwing a ball. Learning the muscle movements used to dance, run, skate, and swim takes practice.

Kinesiologists study how your muscles learn. They have found that learning movements involves watching someone move, picturing yourself doing the moves, and then practicing the moves yourself. Your brain and body work together to create nerve pathways that send signals from your brain to your muscles. Just as your brain memorizes new words and math formulas, your muscles learn new movements.

Potential Energy in Balls

You will need:

- Large, heavy ball such as a basketball
- Small, light tennis ball

1. Hold the two balls together, with the tennis ball on top of the basketball. As you hold the balls in the air, the balls have potential energy.
2. Let go of both balls at exactly the same time.

3. Observe and record what happens. When the two balls hit the ground, the tennis ball bounces off the basketball and back up into the air. Why does this happen?

As they fall, the potential energy of both balls changes into kinetic energy—the energy of movement. The kinetic energy depends on the speed of the ball and its weight. The two balls collide just after hitting the ground. The tennis ball flies higher into the air, because much of the larger amount of kinetic energy in the heavier basketball was transferred to the smaller tennis ball.

3

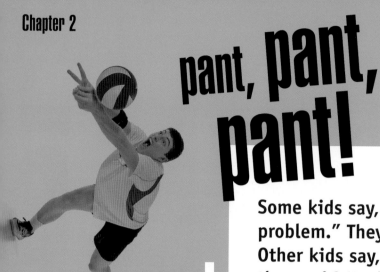

pant, pant, pant!

Some kids say, "20 laps? No problem." They run like gazelles. Other kids say, "Jog around the track? You've got to be kidding!" They find it hard to make it around the block. Most kids are somewhere in between. So why break a sweat? What good does it do to knock yourself out? Ask your lungs. Ask your heart.

Carbon dioxide out, oxygen in!

When you gasp for breath at the end of a sprint, your lungs are rapidly taking in oxygen and passing out CO_2.

What Makes You Gasp for Breath?

Did you ever run wind sprints? Maybe you just watched as someone else did. An athlete jogs for a while and then suddenly puts an all-out effort into running as fast as possible for a short distance. Then back to jogging. The athlete jogs and sprints, jogs and sprints … until he or she is winded, bent over, and gasping for breath.

Wind Sprints

Wind sprints build up an athlete's ability to run or play harder and longer. But athletes doing wind sprints are not the only people who get out of breath. An out-of-shape student who jogs a block to get to school on time can arrive winded and gasping for air.

Athletes train their respiratory systems to be more efficient by carrying out wind sprints.

Gasping in both physically fit people and out of shape people involves two of the many gases that make up air. They are oxygen and carbon dioxide. These gases must be kept in balance in your blood. Not having enough oxygen and having too much carbon dioxide in your bloodstream will make you winded. It is the job of your lungs and respiratory system to help control the levels of these gases in your blood.

Take a Breather!

You will need:
- Ceramic pot
- Water
- Chopped red cabbage
- Strainer
- 2 clear plastic glasses
- Drinking straw

1. Fill a heatproof ceramic pot with water.

2. Boil the red cabbage in the pot. (Uncoated aluminum pots will not work because aluminum reacts with the natural acids in cabbage.)

3. Place a strainer over a glass and pour in half of the red cabbage juice.

4. Again using a strainer, pour the remaining red cabbage juice into the other glass. (You will have two glasses with purple liquid.)

5. Put a straw into one glass. Blow air through the straw, and bubble it through the purple juice.

6. Observe and record what happened.

The purple cabbage juice that you blew air through turned pink. The juice in the glass you left untouched stayed the same color.

Why is that? The air that you blow out of your lungs contains a gas called carbon dioxide, which is a waste product produced by your body. The carbon dioxide in your breath reacts with the cabbage juice, producing an acid. The acid turns the purple juice pink.

Your Body's Windbags

Your lungs are at the center of your respiratory system. There is one lung on each side of your chest. Each one looks like a big, pink sponge, because it is made of tissue that is full of holes. The holes are tiny chambers, called alveoli, which hold air. The ribs form a cage of bones around your chest that protects the lungs.

Whether you are sleeping and breathing lightly or playing dodgeball and breathing hard, air goes in and out of your body the same way. When you take a breath, air flows through your nose or mouth, whooshes past your larynx (voice box), and into a system of tubes that leads into your lungs. The first and largest tube is your trachea (windpipe). The windpipe branches out into two smaller tubes called bronchi. One bronchus enters each lung. Like an upside-down tree, each bronchus branches out to form smaller and smaller tubes inside the lung. This system of tubes is called the bronchial tree. The smallest branches lead to respiratory units that contain about 20 alveoli.

When you lift weights, you work more than the muscles in your arms—your entire respiratory system works hard too.

Up, down, in, out!

Asthma Doesn't Stop Me!

Former National Football League halfback Jerome Bettis is fifth on the NFL's all-time rushing list—he rushed 13,662 yards in his career. You need a good pair of lungs to do this. But Bettis was a remarkable athlete because he suffers from the respiratory condition asthma. People with asthma suffer shortness of breath because the walls of their airways tighten up if they become irritated. Exercise can trigger this, so some people with asthma struggle with sports and other physical activities.

Bettis did not let his asthma get in the way of a successful career. He controlled his asthma with medication. He also trained hard to increase his lung capacity through aerobic exercise and avoided anything that might trigger an attack.

In action Jerome Bettis (36) is a powerhouse of strength. It is impossible to tell that he has asthma.

Gasping: The Great Gas Swap

Blood flowing through tiny blood vessels, called capillaries, in the alveoli swap oxygen for carbon dioxide. The oxygen comes from the air you inhale. When you take a breath, the diaphragm and chest muscles expand the volume of your chest. The lungs get bigger as they fill with air. The air, and the oxygen it contains, passes through the bronchial tree to the alveoli. The walls of the alveoli are very thin—oxygen molecules can pass right through them and into blood in the capillaries. This oxygen-rich blood flows around your body. Cells use the oxygen in blood to burn food molecules for energy.

At the same time, blood vessels deliver waste carbon dioxide from your body to the alveoli. The CO_2 passes from the blood, through the alveoli, and into the lungs. When you breathe out, your lungs expel the CO_2 into the air.

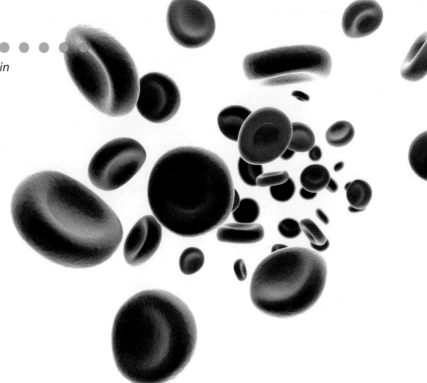

Your lungs take in oxygen but you can thank your millions of red blood cells for transporting it around your body.

Every time you run, your body uses up a lot more oxygen than when you walk.

Normally this gas swap goes along smoothly as you breathe in and out. However, when you exercise, such as when you run to school or do wind sprints, your body's need for oxygen greatly increases. Cells in your muscles work much harder. They use more oxygen to burn more food molecules for energy. Your lungs need to take in more oxygen from air. At the same time, your muscle cells give off more CO_2. The gas balance in your blood tips to more CO_2 and less oxygen. You breathe harder and faster, trying to take in more and more oxygen. When your chest muscles and lungs are working as hard as they can to take in oxygen and get rid of CO_2, you start to gasp for breath. You continue to gasp until the balance between CO_2 and oxygen gets back to normal.

By carrying the oxygen they need to breathe in a tank, divers can explore beneath the ocean's surface.

Breathing Under Water

Water contains dissolved oxygen just as air does. So why can't you breathe water when you swim under water? Land animals have lungs and can only breathe air. It takes gills to get the dissolved oxygen out of water. Fish and many other water creatures have gills. Water flows over gills, and the oxygen in the water enters the blood. At the same time, carbon dioxide in the blood flows out through the gills into the water.

People have found ways to breathe oxygen under water. A swimmer around a shallow coral reef can watch colorful fish while breathing through a tube called a snorkel. Scuba divers carry tanks of pressurized air on their backs and breathe through hoses.

A Pump Made of Muscle

Another major player in the wind sprint story is the heart—a muscular pump inside your chest, between your two lungs. It is hollow so it can fill up with blood. Each time your heart beats, it forces blood out into your body. The heart and respiratory system work together. The heart pumps blood carrying oxygen from your lungs to every cell in your body.

The blood travels through an amazing network of blood vessels called the circulatory system. Blood vessels called arteries carry oxygen-rich blood out to all parts of the body. Blood vessels called veins carry blood rich in CO_2 back to the heart.

The heart has four chambers and two sides, which do different jobs. The right side pumps blood collected by the veins out to the lungs. This blood picks up more oxygen from the air. The left side pumps oxygen-rich blood from the lungs around the body.

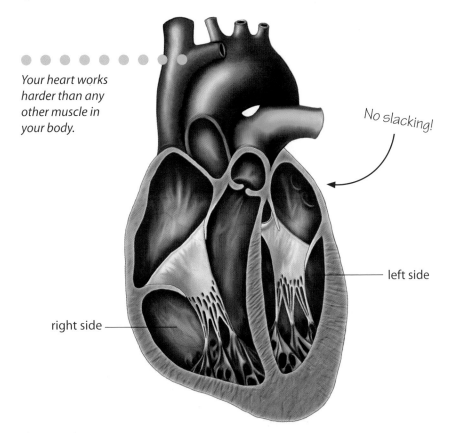

Your heart works harder than any other muscle in your body.

No slacking!

left side

right side

23

The Beat

How fast the heart beats depends on how old a person is and whether he or she is in good physical shape. An infant's heart can beat up to 120 times a minute. The heart of an average adult beats from 60 to 100 times a minute. Teens and adults who are in good shape have slower heart rates. Athletes can have heart rates as low as 40 beats per minute.

You don't have to even think about your heart beating. It beats automatically. Your heart is controlled by a part of your nervous system called the autonomic nervous system. If you are exercising or playing a sport, the autonomic nervous system increases your heart rate. If you are resting, the autonomic nervous system makes your heart beat more slowly.

When you chill out with your friends, your heart takes a rest too and beats more slowly.

Feel and See a Heart Beat

You will need:
- Drinking straw
- Modeling clay
- Partner

1. Find your partner's pulse on the wrist or neck area. Feel for the pulse with two fingers, but not your thumb.

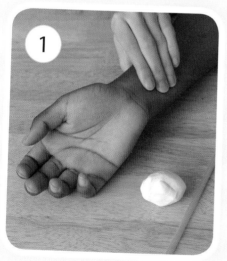

2. Count the number of beats that you feel over 20 seconds. Multiply the result by three to find your partner's heart rate per minute.

3. Press some modeling clay on the place where you located the pulse.

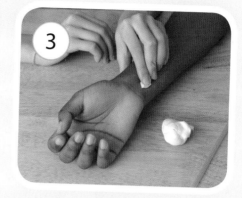

4. Insert the drinking straw into the modeling clay.

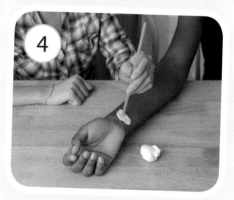

5. Observe and record what happens. Can you see your partner's heartbeat? If so, count the beats (over 20 seconds again) to figure out his or her heart rate. Now have your partner figure out your heart rate. How does your resting heart rate compare with your partner's? How does it compare with the average?

lift what?

Ummph! Oooph! Argh! Clang! Listen to weight lifters in the gym! Not everyone wants to bench-press 250 pounds (110 kilograms). In fact, most kids don't need a weight-training program to become fit and strong. Playing games and doing push-ups, pull-ups, or other exercises is usually enough. So why talk weights? Because everyone has, and needs, muscles. And gym class is a lot about strengthening muscles.

When you do push-ups you give your arm and shoulder muscles an excellent workout.

Playing music would be impossible without muscles.

Your Muscle Collection

Your body has three basic kinds of muscles. You've got skeletal, smooth, and heart muscles. All muscles make parts of your body move, but the three muscle types move different body parts.

Bone Movers

Skeletal muscles hold together the bones that make up your skeleton. These muscles cover your arms, legs, chest, back, abdomen, neck, and face. They make your arm bend and your legs walk or run, and they help you hold a pencil, chew your food, play a musical instrument, and even wink your eye.

The biggest skeletal muscles are in your arms and legs. These muscles bend your knees and elbows. Like all skeletal muscles, they work in pairs. Your upper arm, for example, has a pair of muscles called biceps and triceps. The biceps is on the front of your upper arm, and the triceps is on the back of your arm. When the biceps contracts, the muscle becomes shorter and thicker, bending the elbow to raise your lower arm. At the same time, the triceps relaxes. When the triceps contracts to lower the arm, the biceps relaxes.

FACT!

Move It!

Skeletal muscles usually move only when you tell them to. Suppose you want to run. Your brain tells your leg muscles to contract and get going. A signal from your brain travels along a network of nerves to the skeletal muscles in your legs—and you start running.

Fish Man

true tales

If you're a strong swimmer, you might think swimming 165 yards (150 meters) is a piece of cake. But imagine swimming that distance under water—in one breath! Free diver Carlos Coste set a world record by doing exactly that. Coste, who has been practicing free diving for 12 years, swam the distance equal to the length of three Olympic-size swimming pools under water in a cave in Yucatan, Mexico. The swim took Coste two minutes and 30 seconds—no problem for Coste, though, because he can hold his breath for an amazing seven minutes!

During such a feat, the human body adapts to the conditions. This is a reflex that occurs when the body detects that the face is submerged. The heart rate drops and blood vessels shrink and direct blood to essential organs such as the heart, lungs, and brain. In addition, more red blood cells are released to deliver oxygen to cells. Blood plasma fills the lungs' blood vessels to prevent the lungs from shrinking.

Free divers train their bodies to cope with the strain of diving to great depths under water with no oxygen supply.

28

Smooth Movers

Smooth muscles make up the walls of the stomach, bladder, intestines, and other body organs. They also line the walls of veins and arteries. You do not exercise smooth muscles in gym class. Smooth muscles contract and relax without your ever knowing it. They are controlled by the autonomic nervous system. Smooth muscles operate slowly by contracting and relaxing with a regular rhythm. One job of smooth muscles is to help digest food by churning it around in your stomach and pushing it through your intestines.

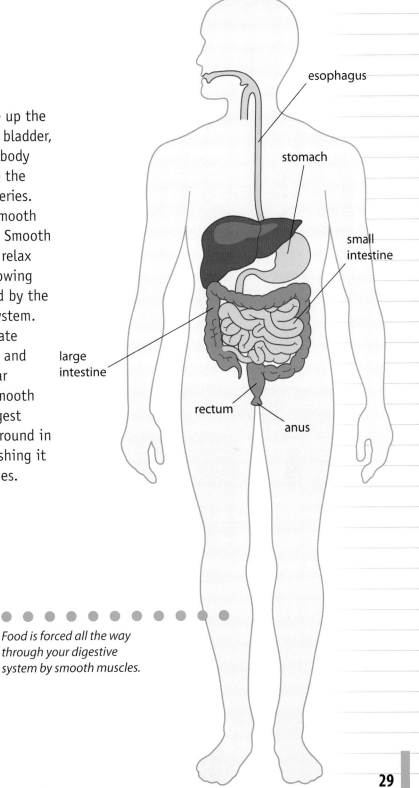

esophagus

stomach

small intestine

large intestine

rectum

anus

Food is forced all the way through your digestive system by smooth muscles.

Blood Pumpers

Heart muscle, also called cardiac muscle, makes your heart tick. This muscle forms the walls of your heart. Cardiac muscle is also controlled by the autonomic nervous system. You can feel your heart beat, but you do not have to think about it. Cardiac muscles contract and relax to pump blood around your body.

Gym activities affect how fast your heart beats. When you play basketball or run around the track, your heart beats faster. Cardiac muscles force more oxygen-rich blood out to skeletal muscles and other body parts. Skeletal muscles work harder when you run or play games and need more oxygen to burn food molecules for energy.

Your heart picks up the pace when you play basketball and other sports.

See How Jogging Affects Your Heart Rate

You will need:
- Watch
- Stopwatch
- Paper and pen for recording results

3. Jog for five minutes.

1. Find your pulse.

4. Stop and find your pulse.

2. Record your heart rate at rest. (Record over 20 seconds, then multiply by three to get the heart rate per minute.)

5. Record your heart rate as before.

6. Repeat this activity three times. When was your heart beating the fastest? When was your heart beating the slowest? Explain what you think caused your heart rate to change and why.

Inside Your Muscles

Muscles are made up of hundreds or thousands of cells called muscle fibers. Skeletal muscle fibers are shaped like long, thin cylinders. Under a microscope the cylinders look as if they had light and dark stripes. The stripes are actually overlapping thick and thin strands that scientists call striations. The striations make skeletal muscles contract.

Most body cells have one central part called the nucleus. Skeletal muscle cells have many nuclei. The nuclei contain substances that repair or replace worn out parts of the hard-working muscle fiber. Skeletal muscle fibers also have parts that produce large amounts of energy from food and oxygen.

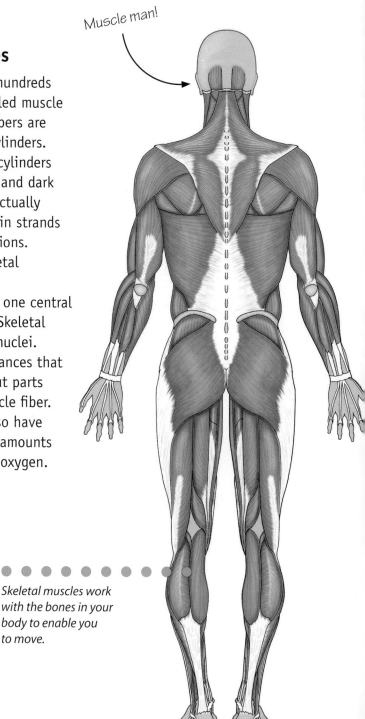

Muscle man!

Skeletal muscles work with the bones in your body to enable you to move.

32

Smooth muscle fibers are smaller than skeletal muscle fibers and do not have any light and dark stripes. All the smooth muscle fibers in an organ contract and relax together.

Heart muscle has long, cylinder-shaped fibers, with light and dark stripes. Controlled by the autonomic nervous system, all the fibers of heart muscle contract at the same time.

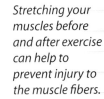

Stretching your muscles before and after exercise can help to prevent injury to the muscle fibers.

Making Strong Muscles

You can exercise to strengthen your skeletal muscles and heart muscles. Lifting weights or doing push-ups or pull-ups makes skeletal muscles grow bigger and stronger. You do these muscle-building exercises for short periods several days a week. The exercises cause the nuclei in skeletal muscle fibers to make more thick and thin stripes.

Exercises done for longer periods three to six days a week build endurance. Running, bicycling, and swimming for 30 minutes to an hour increase the ability of skeletal muscle fibers to create energy. Exercises that make your muscles work harder for longer periods of time are called aerobic exercises.

Aerobic means "with oxygen." When you do aerobic exercise, you breathe faster and more deeply. You inhale more oxygen, which goes from your lungs into your blood and on to your muscles. The increased oxygen in your muscle fibers burns more food molecules to produce more energy.

Aerobics classes force your lungs to work hard.

34

Steroids: More Than Scandals

If you read sports stories in newspapers or on the Web or watch sports news on TV, you may have heard about athletes who take steroids. Steroid use by athletes is banned, and it can seriously damage their health. The steroids abused by some athletes and body builders are called anabolic steroids. These drugs are made in laboratories and increase muscle strength and body weight. There are many kinds of natural steroids, however, that are produced by animals and plants. These steroids play useful roles. Human bodies produce sex hormones. Sex steroids regulate the development of male and female features.

Athletes in many competitions must be tested for steroid abuse.

you don't have to walk a tightrope

Did you ever see a circus performer walk a tightrope? Did you ever see a wading bird standing on one leg? Both need good balance. Some kids in gymnastics have such a good sense of balance that they can do handstands and other routines on a narrow balance beam. Don't feel bad if your balance isn't good enough for walking a tightrope. Just remember that good balance is important for many everyday activities. You learned to balance yourself on two legs when you learned to walk. You learned to balance your body on two wheels when you learned to ride a bike. Balance keeps you from falling over. And if you trip, you can regain your balance.

Gymnasts spend years perfecting their ability to balance.

Balance in Your Ears

Just as you have senses of hearing, vision, touch, and smell, you have a sense of balance. Your sense of balance is provided by your vestibular system, which is inside your ears.

If you could make yourself small enough to fit inside a human ear, you would find yourself in a maze of bones. Inside your ears are many passages and chambers. You would need a map to find your way around.

The map would show an outer ear, a middle ear, and an inner ear. Sound waves enter the opening into the ear and travel through the outer ear to a membrane called the eardrum. Beyond the eardrum lies the middle ear, which contains the bones involved in hearing. Beyond the middle ear is the inner ear, which is also called the bony labyrinth. It has three main parts with magical sounding names—the vestibule, semicircular canals, and cochlea. Only one part, the cochlea, is for hearing.

The business of balance is done in the vestibule and semicircular canals. The job of the vestibule is to keep track of your head's position. Is your head turned to one side, tipped up or down, or hanging upside down?

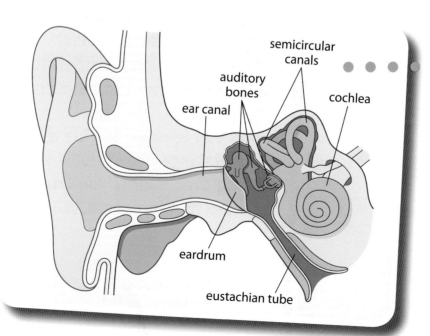

semicircular canals

auditory bones

ear canal

cochlea

eardrum

eustachian tube

Your ear is made up of a series of connecting tubes through which sound waves travel.

Hairy, Scary Vestibule

You would probably be spooked by two baglike sacs in the vestibule. These sacs, called the utricle and the saccule, look like something you might see in a scary Halloween movie. They are lined with sensory receptors, called hair cells, which stick out from the surface. A gellike substance covers the hair cells. Tiny crystals inside the gel would catch your eye. When the head moves, these tiny crystals slide around like bits of paper and metal in a kaleidoscope. As the crystals move, they pull on the gel and the hair cells. The hair cells are attached to nerves that send signals to the brain. If the head leans to the left, the hair cells send signals to the brain that say something like, "Hey! We're tilting to the left!"

When someone calls your name, the hair cells in your ear tell your brain to have you turn to face the person speaking to you.

Behind the vestibule you would find three semicircular canals. Two canals are vertical. The third canal is horizontal. Each canal contains a fluid-filled tube. Each tube has a pouch at one end, with hair cells attached to nerves. The semicircular canals detect when your head turns. When you turn your head to look at something, changes in the fluid in the canals cause the hair cells to send nerve signals that tell your brain, "Hey! We're turning to the right!"

FACT!

Head Over Heels

Your inner ear works overtime when you do a somersault. You start with your head tucked and facing your belly button. As your body rotates, your feet are where your head used to be. As you continue to roll, your body comes back to its normal position. All the while, the fluid and crystals in your inner ear are keeping track of your head's positions to help you keep your balance.

When you tilt your body, it changes the fluid in your ear canals. This sends a message to your brain to tell it you are moving.

We're on the move!

Feeling Dizzy

true tales

One morning when Andy tried to get up out of bed, he nearly fell over. He lay back down again, but still felt dizzy. He hadn't taken anything that might have affected his balance. When Andy still felt dizzy two days later, he went to the emergency room.

Andy told a doctor it felt as if he were drifting to one side when he walked, and he felt as if he were falling over. He'd walked into things a few times and bruised his knee on a table. The doctor checked his ears and diagnosed him with labyrinthitis. This infection of the inner ear distorted the balance signals in Andy's brain. Andy had to have therapy to help his brain learn to adapt. After several months, he was back to normal.

The Brain Works It Out

Your inner ears alone cannot keep your balance. The vestibular system must work with other body parts to keep you upright. Your eyes send information to your brain about the changing scenery as your head moves. Your muscles send information to your brain about the position of your arms and legs as they move. Your brain processes the data to help you keep your balance. The instructions it sends out to your muscles have a lot to do with gravity.

When an ice skater spins in a circle on the ice, she uses gravity to help her complete the move.

The sun's mass is enormous and is responsible for the gravitational pull that forces all the planets in our solar system to orbit the sun.

Gravity and Your Balance

Gravity is a major force in the universe. It holds the planets in orbit around the sun. It brings you back down to the ground when you jump up to catch a ball. Gravity is a force between objects that have mass. Mass is a measure of the quantity of material that any object is made of. Earth has mass. Your gym shorts have mass. You have mass as well.

The force of gravity is greater in objects with more mass. More massive objects pull less massive objects toward them. The sun has more mass than Earth, so its gravity keeps Earth in orbit around it. Earth has more mass than a human body, so it pulls even the best basketball players back down no matter how high they jump for the ball. You experience the pull of Earth's gravity as weight. The more mass your body contains, the more you weigh.

Earth's gravity is always pulling you toward the center of the planet. The center of gravity is the point where an object is in balance. Your body also has a center of gravity. The posture of your body—and its center of gravity—changes as your arms, legs, and head move. These changes affect your balance.

Balancing Act

Try to balance a pencil by its point on your finger or your nose.

You will need:
- Pencil, sharpened to a point
- 2 pieces of wire
- 2 clothespins

1. Place a sharpened pencil by its point on your finger or your nose. Observe and record what happens.

2. Attach one end of each wire to a clothespin.

3. Attach the other end of each wire to the pencil.

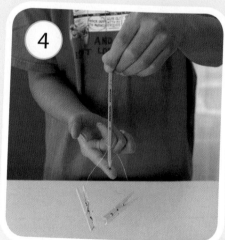

4. Place the pencil by its point on your finger or your nose. Move the clothespins until you find a place that allows the pencil to balance on your finger or nose without holding it. Form a hypothesis to explain why you can balance the pencil.

What happened? Attaching clothespins to the pencil with the wires lowered the pencil's center of gravity. It is easier to balance an object when its center of gravity is lower.

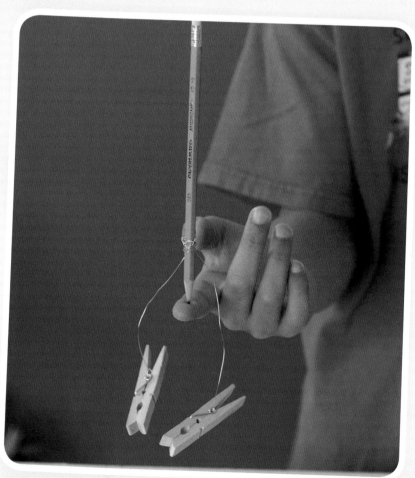

Balance on a Teeter-totter

Picture a playground teeter-totter. This will help you see how the center of gravity works. A teeter-totter is a board balanced on a center point called a pivot. If two kids weighing exactly the same sit on each end, the board will balance straight across the center point. The center of gravity will be at the center of the board. If a heavy adult replaces one kid, the end with the adult will tilt toward the ground. This is because the adult's body has more mass. The kid (whose body has less mass) will be stuck up in the air. The center of gravity shifts from the center of the board toward the end where the adult sits.

The mass of an adult will force a child up into the air on a teeter-totter.

44

When a football player hunches his body, it keeps his center of gravity closer to the ground, which helps him to balance.

The center of gravity in a human body is harder to figure out, but the idea is the same. When the vestibular system and other senses tell the brain that the body is tilting dangerously, the brain sends signals to the muscles. These are instructions that tell you how to move your body to shift your center of gravity to restore balance.

Suppose a gymnast walking on a balance beam starts to fall toward one side or the other. To keep from falling, the gymnast's brain tells her to squat down. A football linebacker spreads his feet out and hunches down before the quarterback hands off the ball. These athletes are lowering their centers of gravity to keep their balance.

FACT!

Winning with Gravity

Scientific research indicates that an athlete's center of gravity may help him or her set records. A study found that the higher the center of gravity, the faster a sprinter is likely to be. Many great sprinters are of West African descent. Their torsos are shorter and their limbs longer than those of other athletes, giving them a higher center of gravity. Sprinters of West African descent run about 1.5 percent faster than other athletes.

Two Kinds of Balance

As far as your body is concerned, there are two kinds of balance—dynamic balance and static balance. Dynamic balance involves movement. Static balance involves staying still for a time and keeping your center of gravity over a fixed base of support. Your base of support is usually your feet and how far apart they are.

The force of gravity acts on all parts of your body all the time. Your body's center of gravity moves to reach a state of balance where your center of gravity is over the base of support.

Several factors affect your balance when playing sports. The size of the base of support affects your center of gravity. Holding your body straight above your feet helps with static balance. If you drew a line through the center of your body and a line across the position of your feet, they would intersect right in the middle of the space between your feet. This is the spot that is best for static balance.

Widely placed feet give a tennis player a solid base of support while she waits to receive the ball.

The farther apart you plant your feet, the easier it is to keep your balance. This is why football linemen and tennis players plant their feet far apart. They are ready to react to any player or ball that comes from any direction.

It is easier to maintain dynamic balance when your body's center of gravity is lower. Crouching or squatting lowers the center of gravity. Gymnasts doing balance beam routines have a small base of support, because their feet must be close together. However gymnasts walking a narrow beam crouch to regain balance.

Big Toes

On most people's feet, the second toe is the longest. But if your big toe is longer, you have a natural advantage in skiing, sprinting, and certain other sports. With a longer big toe, you can more readily lean your full body weight onto it. In skiing, planting the big toe is a must for cutting an edge in the snow. Sprinters also need a firmly grounded big toe to accelerate quickly. Your big toe can exert about twice as much force as your second toe.

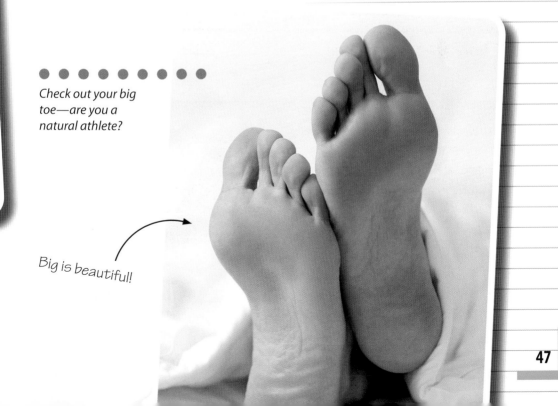

Check out your big toe—are you a natural athlete?

Big is beautiful!

your body as bungee cord

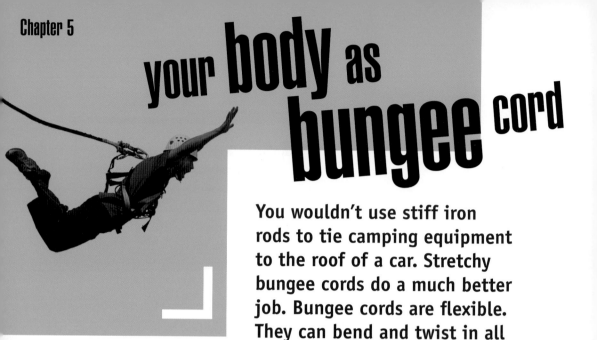

You wouldn't use stiff iron rods to tie camping equipment to the roof of a car. Stretchy bungee cords do a much better job. Bungee cords are flexible. They can bend and twist in all directions without breaking. Your body also needs to bend, twist, pivot, and rotate. Your body needs to be flexible so that it can move around.

Ballet dancers have trained their bodies to be extremely flexible. This allows them to twist and bend into extraordinary positions.

The human bungee!

Body parts called joints allow your body to move and be flexible. Medical scientists define flexibility as the ways in which it is possible for any joint of the body to move. How far a joint can move in various directions is called its range of motion.

What's That Joint?

A joint connects two or more bones. Some joints do not move. These joints act like shock absorbers.

They absorb the shock from blows to the bones they connect. The bones that make up your skull, for example, have fixed joints.

By absorbing shocks, these fixed joints keep your skull bones from breaking if, for example, a softball hits you in the head. But most joints do move. The body has several kinds of moveable joints.

Types of Moving Joints

Hinge joints are located where the ends of bones meet and fit together. The bones that they connect can swing back and forth in one direction, just as a door swings back and forth on its hinges. Joints at the knee and knuckles are types of hinge joints. Hinge joints let you bend or straighten your arms, legs, and fingers.

Pivot joints let the bones they connect move with a rotating motion. The pivot joint in your neck enables you to nod and turn your head from side to side.

Ball-and-socket joints let the bones they connect twist and turn and swing around. In these joints one bone ends in a big round ball. The other bone has a cuplike hollow place called a socket, into which the ball sits. Hip and shoulder joints are ball-and-socket joints.

Gliding joints allow one bone to slide over another. These joints join bones with flat surfaces. Some bones in the wrists and ankles have gliding joints.

Some places where bones meet have more than one kind of joint. For example, your elbow has a hinge joint and a pivot joint. Your thumb has a one-of-a-kind joint called a saddle joint. This joint means your thumb can move from side to side. It can also work with your fingers to grasp things.

The ball-and-socket joint in a baseball player's shoulder allows him to rotate his arm to throw a baseball.

Bones as Simple Machines

You will need:
- Table and chair
- Plastic bucket with a handle
- Partner

1. Seated at the table, stretch your arm out so that your elbow is on the table and your hand is over the table edge, palm out.

2. Have your partner place the bucket handle in your hand.

3. Without letting your elbow leave the table, raise your forearm.

4. Observe and record what happens to the bucket.
5. Draw what this would look like if parts were made of wood, instead of your arm.

Compare how your arm works to the way a simple machine works.

Tendons and Ligaments

Did you ever see a soccer player lying on the field holding his or her leg? The player may have injured a tendon or ligament. Tendons and ligaments are tough bands or sheets of tissue that connect parts of the skeletal system.

Tendons connect muscles to bones. A muscle pulls on a tendon to make a bone move. Ligaments connect bones to form joints. Ligaments attach only to bones.

Sports injuries often involve damage to ligaments and tendons. Stretching a ligament too far causes a sprain. Falls or movements that twist joints and their ligaments may also cause sprains.

Strains are injuries to muscles or tendons. Strains occur when a muscle or tendon stretches too far. A muscle that gets stretched while it is contracting can also be strained. Exercises that increase flexibility can help prevent strains and sprains in gym class or on the sports field.

Most exercise classes include a warm-up and a cool-down with stretches to help prevent damage to the muscles.

Loosening Up

You probably start gym class with some warm-up exercises. You might bend down and touch your toes. You might stretch your arms high above your head and tilt to the left and right. Stretching increases the flexibility of your joints.

Many good things come from training your body to be more flexible.

Joints that are flexible have a greater range of motion. They let your arms, legs, and head move farther up or down and to the left or right. Stretching makes muscles, tendons, and ligaments more like bungee cords than steel rods. When these tissues are flexible, they are less likely to be injured. Flexible muscles are less likely to be sore after doing exercises.

Yoga is an excellent way to maintain flexibility of the joints and lengthen and stretch the muscles.

S-t-r-e-t-c-h!

Improve Your Flexibility

In this experiment you will do a seven-minute stretching program over several weeks to improve your body's flexibility.

You will need:
- You!

1. Start by loosening the muscles in your neck. Tilt your head to one side and hold for 30 seconds. Switch sides.

2. Stretch your upper body. Stand with your feet shoulder-width apart and your arms pointed outward. Make small circles with your arms. Gradually widen the circles. Repeat the process but rotate your arms in the opposite direction.

3. Stretch your legs. Stand up straight and lean in to touch your toes. Remember to keep your legs straight. Hold the position for 30 seconds.

4. Finish off by stretching your back. Kneel on all fours and arch your back, tucking in your tummy and rounding out your shoulders. Hold the position for 30 seconds. Then reverse the pose, relaxing your back but pushing your tummy toward the floor. Hold this position for 30 seconds.

Use the Internet to find more stretches you can do to improve your flexibility. Over time your body will feel more supple. If you couldn't touch your toes before, you might be able to now!

looking good, feeling good

According to the old saying, an apple a day keeps the doctor away. Sure, good nutrition is essential for good health, but so is exercise. A brisk walk or jog or bike ride might be just as good as an apple to keep you healthy and free from disease.

Exercise and Healthy Hearts

Medical scientists keep finding more reasons to put the lessons you learn in gym class to work in everyday life. Regular aerobic exercise can keep your heart and blood vessels healthy. Research shows that exercise can help prevent heart disease. Heart disease is usually caused by damage to blood vessels in the heart. Fatty deposits called plaque build up on the inner walls of arteries in the heart. The walls of the arteries get stiff and thick, and the arteries clog up. Doctors call this condition atherosclerosis. If an artery gets totally blocked, blood cannot reach parts of the heart to deliver vital oxygen and nutrients. The result is a heart attack.

A healthy diet works hand in hand with exercise to keep you in good shape.

Exercise and Strong Bones

Exercise also helps make your bones strong. This can help prevent a bone disorder called osteoporosis. As people get older, their bones do not produce enough new bone tissue to replace worn-out bone. Bones become fragile and break easily. Vigorous exercise, such as running or brisk walking, along with good nutrition, can help prevent osteoporosis.

Many doctors advise young people to continue regular exercise as they get older to help prevent osteoporosis.

Keep on running!

Testing Sports Materials

Some sports equipment, such as bicycles, must be made of strong and elastic materials. A material with the property of elasticity bends or stretches and then returns to its original shape. Yield strength is the amount of force needed to permanently bend a material out of shape. Ultimate strength is the force needed to break a material. Test the properties of elasticity, yield strength, and ultimate strength in various materials.

You will need:
● Rubber band
● Plastic ballpoint pen
● Wooden pencil
● Metal paper clip

1. Make a chart with four columns.
2. In column one list the material that each object is made of. In the other three columns, list the properties you will test for.

Material	Elasticity	Yield strength	Ultimate strength

3. Try bending and stretching each object.
4. Record the results in your chart.

Which material—rubber, plastic, wood, or metal—would be best to use to make the various parts of a bicycle?

Sugar Isn't Always Sweet

Sugar is a big problem when it comes to diabetes. This disease is caused by the body's inability to regulate simple sugar, glucose, in the blood. Normally a hormone called insulin helps cells take sugar out of the bloodstream. In people with diabetes, something goes wrong with blood-sugar control.

Type 1 diabetes is caused by the destruction of cells that produce insulin in an organ called the pancreas. Type 2 diabetes is caused by the body's inability to use insulin properly. Sugar builds up in the blood and can cause health problems, including blindness, kidney failure, poor blood circulation, and eventually death.

Not as sweet as it looks . . .

Eating too much sugary food can make you gain weight. People who are overweight have a higher risk of developing Type 2 diabetes. The bodies of people with diabetes cannot remove sugar from their blood effectively.

Full-body swimsuits made of high-tech material were thought to provide an unfair advantage in races.

The good news is that researchers have found that exercise helps prevent Type 2 diabetes. Exercise also helps control excessive weight gain—one of the root causes of Type 2 diabetes.

By helping to control weight, exercise is also good for controlling blood pressure. You also feel good after you exercise. Exercise makes the brain release chemicals called endorphins. These chemicals can help you cope with worries about a big test or some other event that's causing you stress. So gym class really is about much more than dodgeball. It is where you can learn a set of skills to help keep you healthy for life.

true tales

Slicker Than Skin

A high-tech material helped swimmers set records until it was banned after the 2008 Beijing Olympics. The super-smooth fabric offers less drag in the water. Surface friction when moving through air or water creates a force called drag. This force slows down a plane through air or a swimmer through water. Working with the National Aeronautics and Space Administration, Speedo USA found a slick fabric and a way of welding seams of the fabric together to make full-body suits.

glossary

alveoli—tiny chambers in the lungs that exchange air and carbon dioxide

biochemistry—the study of chemical reactions in living things

bronchi—tubes that carry air into the lungs and carbon dioxide out

capillaries—the smallest blood vessels

carbon dioxide—a waste product gas exhaled by the lungs

cerebellum—the part of the brain that keeps you balanced

cerebrum—the main part of the brain that does most of the thinking

contract—to shorten or tighten a muscle so that a bone moves

labyrinth—a maze or complex network of passages

kinetic energy—energy that can be transferred by a moving object

larynx—voice box in the throat

ligament—band of tough, flexible tissue that holds a joint together

membrane—a covering or lining

microchip—computer chip; tiny disk of electronic circuits used in computers

nervous system—network of nerve cells and fibers that send signals to all parts of the body

neuron—a nerve cell

nucleus—central part of a cell

osteoporosis—disease that results in brittle, fragile bones

oxygen—a gas in air that is necessary for animals to breathe

physiology—science of how living things function

receptor—cell that responds to light, sound, or other stimulation

reflexes—actions and responses performed without thinking about them

steroids—natural substances that include hormones and vitamins

tendon—band of tough tissue connecting bone to muscle

vestibular—of the inner ear and sense of balance

additional resources

Read More

Biskup, Agnieszka. *Football: How It Works.*
  Mankato, Minn.: Capstone Press, 2010.

Boudreau, Helene. *Swimming Science.* New York: Crabtree, 2009.

Levine, Shar, and Lesley Johnstone. *Sports Science.*
  New York: Sterling, 2006.

Internet Sites

Use FactHound to find Internet sites
related to this book.
All of the sites on FactHound have
been researched by our staff.

Here's all you do:
Visit *www.facthound.com*
Type in this code:
9780756544850

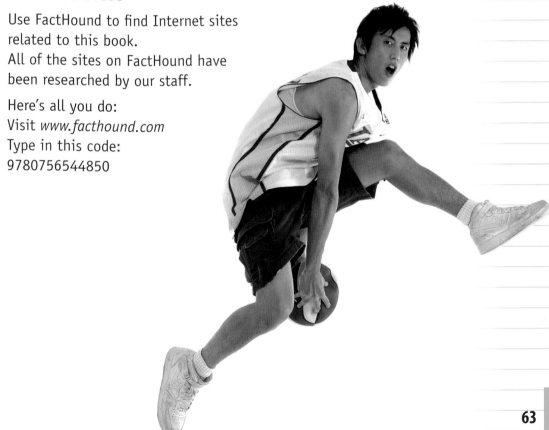

index

About the author:
Darlene R. Stille has combined her love of science and writing to author nearly 100 books for young people. She lives and writes in Michigan.